AGNI-VĀYU-ĀDITYA

THE INDO-EUROPEAN
TRINITY OF FIRE

ALEXANDER JACOB

978-0-6486072-1-2

Agni-Vāyu-Āditya:
The Indo-European Trinity of Fire

Alexander Jacob

Thema Classification: QRD (Hinduism), QRSW (Norse Mythology), QRSG (Greek Mythology), QRSL (Roman Mythology).

MANTICORE PRESS
WWW.MANTICORE.PRESS

CONTENTS

Fig 1. - Georges Dumézil (1898-1988).

PROLOGUE

In the field of Indo-European comparative mythology Georges Dumézil holds a special position on account of his well-known hypothesis of trifunctionality in ancient Indo-European societies.[1] The fact of social division into three castes, in India, or into classes, in Germany, is indeed undeniable. However, Dumézil's suggestion that separate castes or classes had separate deities, for instance, is a blatant absurdity:

> below the celestial, royal and highly sacred Jupiter, and below the warlike Mars, the older god Quirinus seems to have been the patron of the Roman people.[2]

Dumézil goes on to extend these distinctions to 'the machinery of the world and of society' as if the gods themselves could be distinguished by the caste to which they belonged:

---

[1]   See, for example, G. Dumézil, *Jupiter, Mars, Quirinus: Essai sur la conception indo-europennes de la societe et sur les origines de Rome*, Paris: Gallimard, 1941, *L'idéologie tripartie des Indo-Européens*, Paris, 1958.

[2]   *Archaic Roman Religion: with an Appendix on the Religion of the Etruscans*, Baltimore, MD: Johns Hopkins University Press, 1996, p.161.

The conceptual religious structure which is manifested in these three hierarchrised terms is now familiar to Indo-Europeanists. It can be observed, with the special peculiarities of each of the societies, among the Indians and Iranians as well as among the ancient Scandinavians and, with more pronounced alterations, among the Celts ... I have proposed, for the sake of brevity, to call this structure 'the ideology of the three functions.' The principal elements and the machinery of the world and of society are here divided into three harmoniously adjusted domains. These are, in descending order of dignity, sovereignty with its magical and juridical aspects and a kind of maximal expression of the sacred; physical power and bravery, the most obvious manifestation of which is victory in war; fertility and prosperity, with all kinds of conditions and consequences ... The 'Jupiter-Mars-Quirinus' grouping ... corresponds to the lists which occur in Scandinavia and in Vedic and pre-Vedic India: Odin, Thor, Freyr; Mitra-Varuna, Indra, Nāsatya.[3]

It is true that correspondences are drawn in the ancient Vedic scriptures between human characteristics and cosmic forces, but these are not a result of contemporary sociological distinctions but rather of an inherent tendency of Indian philosophy, from the Purusha Sūkta of the *Rig Veda,* X, 90 onwards, to allot different sections of the population to different parts of the Cosmic Man according to

---

[3] *Ibid.*

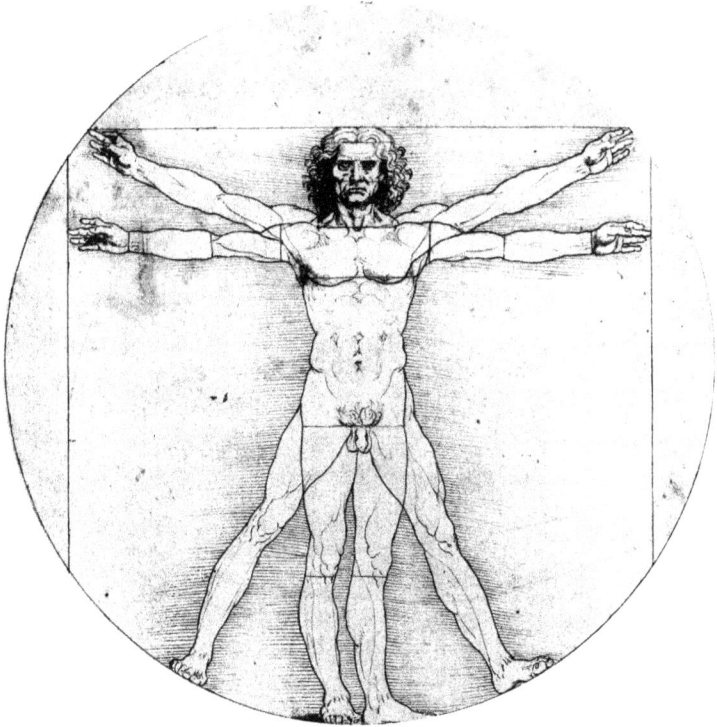

Fig. 2 - Vitruvian Man – Leonardo da Vinci.

their various innate psychological and physical qualities. Thus, we find it stated in *RV* X,90 that

> 12 The Brahman was his mouth, of both his arms was the Rājanya made.
> His thighs became the Vaiśya, from his feet the Śūdra was produced.

and further:

7

13 The Moon was gendered from his mind,
and from his eye the Sun had birth;
Indra and Agni from his mouth were born,
and Vāyu from his breath.
14 Forth from his navel came mid-air [=the
Mid-Region], the sky [Heaven] was fashioned
from his head,
Earth from his feet, and from his car the
regions.

We see that Indra is always identified with physical strength and, consequently, associated with the kshatriya caste. In the description of Varuna, the god of the Earth, and his counterpart Mitra in *RV* VI,68,3, too, Varuna is worshipped as a bearer of 'kshatra' or sovereignty and Mitra as a more brāhmanical figure. However, only the brāhman has specific deities, Indra and Agni, assigned to him in *RV* X,90 since they are equally located in the mouth[4] of the Purusha. The vaisya is associated with the organs of generation (thighs), but there is no reference to a deity in combination with this organ other than the creative Prajāpati aspect of Brahman itself in the *Bhāgavata Purāna* III,6,23. Similarly, since the shūdra is identified with the feet of the Purusha in RV,X,90 as well as the material universe arising from Earth, we must assume the deity associated with this caste is Prithvi (Earth), even though there is no explicit mention of such an association. The gods that rule the various parts of the macrocosmos clearly precede the social distinctions established by the

---

[4] The mouth represents speech, the word (logos), and the goddess Vāk, who is sometimes considered a consort of Brahman and the mother of the Vedas.

Indo-Āryans in Vedic society and do not, as a result of the increasing consolidation of caste distinctions, attach themselves to different castes, as Dumézil suggests. Consequently, it is not possible to establish any tripartite division of the gods according to the social divisions of ancient Indo-European society.

If the sociological trinities proposed by Dumézil may be discarded as artificial, there is nevertheless a definite trinity that is discernible in ancient Indo-European mythologies based on specific phases of the cosmological evolution itself. This will be perceived in a brief review of one significant trinity of ancient Indo-European mythology that is prevalent across Indo-Iranian, Anatolian, and Western Indo-European religions. This is the trinity presented in the familiar liturgical formula of the Indo-Āryans: 'Agni-Vāyu-Āditya' – the Fire of the Earth, the Fire of the Mid-Region of the Stars (our universe), and the Fire of the Heavens (the sun). We will find that the trinities observable in ancient Roman religion, Quirinus-Mars-Diespiter, and in the Germanic lands, Thor-Freyr-Wotan, may also have followed the same classification of deities as in ancient India even though the cosmic dimension of the mythologies in these countries is less distinct.

In order to understand the cosmological basis of all Indo-European mythologies, it may be useful to briefly repeat here the reconstruction of ancient Indo-European cosmogony that I first presented in my study *Ātman: A Reconstruction of the Solar Cosmology of the Indo-Europeans.*[5]

---

[5]   See A. Jacob, Ātman: *A Reconstruction of the Solar Cosmology of the Indo-Europeans,* Hildesheim: Georg Olms, 2005.

At the end of the first cosmic age, the supreme Soul (**Ātman**/Shiva), desirous of creation, acquires through the fervour (**Agni**) of his desire an ideal macroanthropomorphic form as the Purusha. From the nostrils of this macroanthropos emerges the life-breath of the deity, **Vāyu**,[6] in the form of a Boar[7] which recovers the Earth sunk at the bottom of the cosmic ocean during the flood that brought the first cosmic age to a close. The boar/Vāyu then impregnates and spreads Earth, producing, as a result, extended Earth (Prithvi/Gaia) and its "cover" primal Heaven, Brahman (Dyaus/Ouranos/source of the later **Āditya**) in a closely united complex.

However, the temporal concomitant of the rapidly moving Wind-form of the supreme deity,

---

[6] The Germanic **Wotan** must be identified with the Indo-Iranian **Wata**, a companion of Vāyu, the god of 'Wind' (the source of Prāna/life-breath). While Wata is not a clearly defined deity in the Vedas, he is – in the Middle Persian version of Zoroastrianism called Zurvanism (from 'Zurvan', Time) – represented as a companion of Vāyu, and denotes the spatial aspect of the original life-breath or air. Thus, while Vāyu represents the life-breath, Wata is space. In the Avesta's 'Ram Yasht', the chief deity worshipped is Vāyu, who is described as the one who 'goes through the two worlds, Heaven and Earth'.

[7] In the Indic *Bhāgavata Purāna*, the boar is the second, early cosmic, incarnation of the supreme deity (called Vishnu, his solar form) and, in the Avestan Yasht 14, the first form of Verethragna (corresponding to the Indic Vishnu and Indra) is Wata, and the fifth form is as a boar.

In Norse mythology, the boar is associated with the god Freyr and his sister Freyja. Freyr is called Yng in eastern Scandinavia and Freia Ing in England. But Yng or Ygg is an epithet of Wotan too. Thus, while the boar is the form assumed by Vāyu/Wata/Wotan, the breath of the Purusha, to recover and mate with Earth in the original cosmos, in the underworld it becomes the vehicle particularly of Freyr, who represents the revived phallic force of the Purusha.

Shiva/Kāla/Chronos, separates the united Heaven
and Earth by castrating the Purusha, since the
phallus is the instrument of desire as well as of life.
The semen that falls from the castrated phallus of
Heaven impregnates the Purusha bound to Earth
with a Cosmic Egg, from which then emerges the
manifest cosmos constituted of Earth, in the form of
a lotus, crowned with a Heaven of divine Light and
Consciousness (Brahman/Helios). The ruler of this
primal cosmos is Chronos.

This manifest Purusha, or macroanthropos,
crowned with effulgent Light (Brahman/Ouranos)
is, however, shattered by the persistent stormy aspect
(or 'son') of Chronos – Zeus/Indic Ganesha – and
forced to descend into the nether regions of the
"lotus" Earth. Zeus/Ganesha, however, preserves the
castrated phallus of the ideal Man (containing the life
of our yet unmanifested universe) by swallowing it.[8]
In the underworld, where the Purusha lies moribund
as the Lord of Earth (**Varuna**/Aegir/Quirinus)
surrounded by an Ocean (Okeanos), the stormy
and vital aspect of the same force (Zeus/Indra/
Thor) destroys the serpent of material resistance

---

[8]   The commentator of the Orphic Derveni theogony explains
that Zeus indeed swallowed "the sexual organ" [aidion] (see
M.L. West, *Orphic Poems*, p.85). In other versions of the Orphic
theogony, Phanes 'counterpart of Brahman) is said to be devoured
by Zeus (see M.L. West, *op.cit.*, p.88f.) thereby absorbing the
original universe into himself, but we may assume that it is the
phallus of Phanes that is thus consumed. From this Orphic
evidence, we may assume that the Hurrian Teshup, too, finally
swallows this phallus so that the universal life that it contains
moves into his own body. Ganesha is normally depicted with an
elephant's head bearing a phallic trunk and with a "pot-belly"
which contains the entire universe (see S.L. Nagar, *The Cult of
Vinayaka*, N.Delhi: Intellectual Publishing House, 1992, p.115).

Fig. 3 - Ganesha, Lakshmana Temple, Kajuraho, 10th
c. A.D.

that surrounds the Earth, and divides its body into the heaven and earth of our own universe. Imbibing the aphrodisiac juice 'Soma,' which is the essence of the desire that caused Dyaus/Ouranos/Heaven to mate with Earth in the primal cosmos, Indra/ Wotan/Dionysus then rejuvenates the Lord of Earth and the divine phallus, which then rises – between heaven and earth – in the Mid-region of the stars as our **universe**. The entire universe informed by the life-giving force of Soma is now shaped in the form of a "Tree of Life" (Ashvatta/Indra), an analogue of the divine phallus itself, whose roots are in the underworld, trunk and branches in the mid-region, and its peak in heaven.

The chthonic elements of this Tree of Life, however, have to be purified, and this is accomplished by the self-sacrifice of the wind-god (**Vāyu**/Iranian Wata/Wotan) on the universal tree. This done, the seed of the phallus bearing the life and light of the original Cosmic Man is finally free to emerge in our universe as the **sun** (**Āditya**).

We see, therefore, that there are two distinct stages in the evolution of our cosmos, the first marked by the formation of the macroanthropomorphic Purusha, being the primal cosmos ruled by the Titan Chronos, and the second marked by the rise of our universe from the sunken Heaven, Dyaus, in the nether regions of Earth.[9] This universe is ruled by the god Zeus. The divine forces that rule in our universe are related to those that ruled the original cosmos even though their operations and effects are rather

---

[9]   The notion of two cosmic phases is reflected in Plato's *Politicus* 269c-272b, where Socrates outlines the differences between the age of Chronos and that of Zeus.

different. The trinity that is frequently evoked by the brāhmanical priests in India, Agni-Vāyu-Āditya, is one that occurs first in the primal cosmos and then in the Earth. It is the second of these cosmic events that is focused on by the priests in their liturgies. This comprises the forms of fire first as Agni/Varuna in the Earth – where the castrated Heaven lies moribund after his first two violations by Chronos and then by Zeus -, then in the rising universe and solar force as Vāyu-Wotan/Indra/Mitra, and finally as the sun of our system, Āditya/Sūrya-Hvare.

THE SOLAR FORCE

IN THE EARTH, THE MID-REGION
OF THE UNIVERSE, AND HEAVEN

I.

AGNI

The second trinity of Agni-Vāyu-Āditya marks the formation of our sun from the underworld, and it is this sequence that we shall focus on in the present study. The solar force that is contained in the seed of the divine phallus gradually begins to be developed in the underworld into the sun of our system. The developing sun, like the original cosmic Agni, assumes three forms, the first representing Agni, the second Vāyu, while the third is called Āditya. In *KYV* I,3,14, the solar fire Agni is said to be manifest in a trifold form as Agni-Vāyu-Āditya, Agni being the solar force in the underworld of Varuna, Vāyu the fiery life of our universe, and Āditya the sun of the heavens.

The first form of the sun is born of Heaven, that is, the original Dyaus/Ouranos, the castrated Purusha and is, as we have seen, submerged in the Earth. This is **the sun of Earth**. In the Vedic literature, **Agni** is said to have been born in the womb of Earth (*Shatapatha Brāhmana* VII,4,1,8-9). In *KYV* IV,2,2, we get a glimpse also of the form of Agni in the Earth:

> Agni hath cried, like Dyaus thundering,
> Licking the earth, devouring the plants;
> Straightway on earth he shone aflame.

We know that the Anatolian Hittites also distinguished three forms of the sun, the sun-god of earth, the sun-god of the waters, and the sun-god of the heavens. There is, further, a reference in the Hittite Telipinu myth (KUB XVII 10 iv ll8ff)[10] to the "way of the sun-god of the earth" (taknaš ᵈUTU-us), which is contrasted to the "kingly path" (kas lugal) followed by the sun-god of heaven (l.12). The paths of the suns in Hittite religion may be related to the three steps taken by Vishnu through Heaven, the Mid-region and Earth, called paramapada (the supreme step), pitryāna (the step of the *manes*),[11] and devayāna (the step of the gods). If they are, then the way of the sun-god of earth corresponds to the devayāna, the path of the sun-god of the waters to the pitrayāna and the kingly path of the Hittite sun-god of heaven to the paramapada.

It should be noted that, in Hittite, while the fire-god is commonly referred to as ᵈPahhur (from Sumerian pah-har),[12] there are some ritual texts

---

[10] See E. Tenner, "Tages- und Nachtsonne bei den Hethitern," *ZA* 38 (1929), p.189.

[11] The manes are, in *Manusmriti* III,192ff, said to be the offspring of the Seven Sages and from them, in turn, sprang the gods and dānavas.

[12] "Pah-hur/pahhur is clearly the source of the Greek 'pur'=fire. The Sanskrit epithet of Sūrya (the sun), "pāvaka," meaning 'the purifier,' may be related to it, since the sun purifies the seed of the slaughtered first Man in the Iranian cosmogony (see below p.41).

Fig.4 - Vishnu taking one of three colossal steps,
Virupaksha Temple, Hampi, 8th c. B.C.

which refer to ^d**Akni** as well.[13] Agni, in these Hittite texts, seems to be an appellation of Fire in its destructive aspects and related to the Early Dynastic Mesopotamian deity Nergal, who is also characterized by intense brightness. What is especially interesting is that the ritual texts in KBo XI and KBo XIII seem to equate Agni with the sun-god,[14] which must here be the sun-god of the earth.[15]

In the earliest recorded inscription bearing Sanskritic names, the Mitanni treaty between the Mitanni-Hurrian king Šattiwaza and the Hittite king Šuppililiumas I dating from the fourteenth century B.C., we find the names Mitra-Varuna, Indra, and

---

[13] This was first discovered by F. Hrozny, "Un dieu hittite Ak/Nis"; cf. J. Friedrich, "Agniš," *RLA* I:42; F. Sommer, "Review of H. Eheloff", p.688; H.Otten and M. Mayrhofer, "Der Gott Akni, p.545-52. The Sumerian word for fire, Girra, is probably also related to the Sanskrit 'agni,' since the original form of 'agni,' according to SB VI,i,1,xi is 'agri' (see U.C. Pandey, *Cosmogonic Legends of the Brahmanas*, Gorakahpur: Shivaniketan, 1991/2, p.32).

[14] See H. Otten and M. Mayrhofer, "Der Gott Akni in den hethitischen Texten und seine indoarische Herkunft," *OLZ*, 1965, 11/12, p.548.

[15] This close similarity of the Hittite religion to the Indic (represented in the ancient Near East by the Mitanni kingdom) suggests that the Hittites may be considered as part of the Indo-Iranian Āryan culture in spite of their centum language.

Nāsatyas[16] invoked by the writer.[17] We note from the order of the deities, **Mitra-Varuna, Indra, and the Nāsatyas,** that they represent the deities ruling Earth, the Mid-Region of the universe, and Heaven. Mitra-Varuna represent aspects of Agni as sun-god of the Earth. It may be noted that the Hurro-Akkadian version of the Lord of the Waters among the Mitanni is also 'Uruwana' or 'Aruna.' In the Vedic *Gopatha Brāhmana,* I,1,7, Varana[18] is indeed the secret form of the name Varuna,[19] and this repeats the penultimate vowel of both (Mitanni) "Uruwana" and (Gk.) "Ouranos." The form "Aruna" is perhaps related to the Hittite term for "ocean" "arunas,"[20] since Earth is surrounded by a cosmic ocean.

In the Avesta, **Atar** is called a son of the primal god Ahura Mazda (Yasna 62,7). Atar may also be identified with the deity called "Apām Napāt" (child of the waters) who is also equivalent to Agni,

---

[16]   The Nāsatyas, also called Ashvins, are twin sons of the sun, Sūrya.

[17]   The text, CTH 51 and 52 (see D. Yoshida, *Untersuchungen zu den Sonnengottheiten bei den Hethitern,* Heidelberg: Universitätsverlag C. Winter, 1996, p.12; cf. V. Haas, *Geschichte,* p.543) reads "[Dingir Meš]Mitraššiel, [Dingir Meš]Uruwanaššiel, [D]Indar, [Dingir Meš]Našattiyana", where the meaning of the suffix "šiel" is uncertain.

[18]   Following the example of the Latin pronunciation, we may assume that the original Sanskrit of this region also favoured the "u" sound for the phoneme later transcribed with a "v."

[19]   "Being Varana, he is mystically called Varuna, because the gods love mysticism" (see U. Chouduri, *Indra and Varuna in Indian Mythology,* Delhi: Nag Publishers, 1981, p.95).

[20]   See G. Wilhelm, "Meer" in *RLA* VIII:3. Wilhelm suggests that this term is not of Indo-European origin [by which he no doubt means that which is properly called Āryan], but, rather, Hattic.

particularly as the incipient sun. In Zamyad Yasht XIX,37; Fargard XX, Thraetaona[21] is said to battle the monster Asi Dahaka for the possession of the xvarenah. In Zamyad Yasht VIII,45,52, Atar combats the same serpent for the xvarenah, so Thraetona must be closely related to Atar. Atar is the storm-force (Ganesha/Zeus) in the underworld that helps in the formation of the sun of our system. Thraetona may thus be the same as Trita Āptya, who is a form of Agni[22] that helps Indra in his fight against the monstrous Vishvarupa for the release of the solar force (*SB* I,ii,3,1-2). For Thrita, too, is referred to in Yasna IX,10 as smiting the serpent Dahaka, which equates Dahaka with the monstrous Vishvarūpā.[23]

When Thraetona's son Keresaspa takes possession of the xvarenah, he similarly does battle with the serpent as well as with "the golden-heeled Gandareva[24] that was rushing with open jaws, eager to destroy the living world of the good principle" (Yasht XIX,41). When it finally reaches the Vouru-kasha sea, where is no doubt situated the cosmic tree representing the new universe, it is guarded by Apām Napāt (Agni as the child of the waters), who bestows it then to the material world, along with "the waters" and the "mighty Wind" (Wata/Wotan) and the "frawashis [souls][25] of the faithful" (Tir Yasht (VIII), 34).

---

[21]   Thraetona may be related to the Traitona of *RV* I,158,5.

[22]   The three Āptya forms are Ekata ("the first"), Dvita ("the second"), and Trita ("the third") (*SB* I,ii,3,1).

[23]   See below p.34.

[24]   Gandharvas are heavenly singers in the Vedas but included among the enemies of the fire-god in the Avesta.

[25]   The Iranian term "frawashi" is related to the Sanskrit "urwashi" meaning a female spirit.

Varuna-Xvarenah-Quirinus

In the Indic literature (*KB* 18,9) the 'sun' is said to enter the waters and there become **Varuna**. This is not a reference to the setting sun but to the descent of the Heavenly light (Brahman), called Ouranos in ancient Greece and Xvarenah in ancient Iran, into the waters of Earth and the formation of the sun in the 'underworld.' From the Iranian evidence discussed below, we may thus identify Ouranos not as a blue 'sky' but as a golden light or 'glory.' Varuna in the underworld is the Heavenly light Brahman that has been shattered by Kāla/Chronos/Angra Manyu. From the underworld, the solar force rises to the realm of Soma (Mind/Moon) and then emerges as the rising sun, Sūrya/Horus the Younger.

It may be noted that Varuna is identified with Indra in more than one passage in the Vedas. In *RV* IV,42, for instance, Indra calls himself Varuna "I am King Varuna." However, Indra is not exactly the same as Varuna but a warlike form of him since, in *RV* VII, 82,5 we read that "In peace and quiet Mitra waits on Varuna, the Other [Indra] awful, with the Maruts[26] seeks renown." Here Mitra and Indra are both forms of Varuna and contrasted as exemplars of virtue and violence. In *RV* VI,68,3, too, Indra with the mace used against the dragon Vrtra and Mitra are described as companions with contrary characteristics: "One

---

[26]   According to the *BP* VI,18,10ff., the Maruts are the sons, not of Aditi, but of Diti, who, like Aditi, is one of the thirteen wives of Kashyapa. They are borne by Diti as Asuras in order to destroy Indra, chief of the devas. However, Indra succeeds in entering Diti's womb and cuts the foetus into seven parts, which multiply seven-fold to form the forty-nine Maruts, who are later converted into devas by Indra and led by him.

with his might and thunderbolt slays Vrtra; the other (Mitra) as a Sage stands near in troubles" Mitra is typically the "brāhmanical" god, since he is originally the same as Brahman. Indra, on the other hand, is the "kshatriya." Since Varuna is in *RV* IV, 42 called 'King Varuna' and kingship is a kshatriya privilege, we see that Varuna as the fallen Ouranos contains both kshatriya and brāhmanical qualities in himself – which would, as we shall see, contradict Dumézil's interpretation of Quirinus as a god of the third caste.

It has been suggested by P. Kretschmer[27] that the name **Indra** and the Iranian "andra" may be related to the Greek "aner"/man (the Vedic word for man. "nar" is clearly the original to which the Greek has added an initial euphonic "a"). Indra's name is also closely related to the Vedic "ina" and "indriya" meaning strength as well as manliness, similar to the Latin *virtù*.[28] Hittite has a counterpart to this Vedic word in "innarawanza" (XVII 20 II 3, Bo 84 I 25) and its plural "innarawam" (IX 31 I 36 II 6=HT 1 I 29).[29] J. Przyluski[30] also suggested that Inara, the Hittite counterpart of Indra, may derive from the root "nar" ("man"). V. Machek[31] objected that it is not certain that "nar" could be an abbreviated form of "inar." However, the Vedic "ina" may have given the name Inara, just as the Vedic "indriya" (strength) may be

---

[27] "Indra und der hethitische Gott Indra," *Kleinasiatische Forschungen* I (1930), p.307).

[28] See V. Machek, "Name und Herkunft des Gottes Indra," *AO* 12 (1941), pp.146ff.

[29] See K. Laroche, «Recherches sur les noms divins hittites». *RHA* VII, Fasc-45 (1946-7), p.74.

[30] «Inara et Indra», *RHA* V. Fasc.36 (1939), pp.142-46.

[31] *op.cit.*, p.146.

related to Indra. In BP III,6,23, Indra is associated with the arms of the Purusha, indicating that he is particularly identifiable with the strength of the solar force. That is why the full light of Brahman/Āditya in our universe is, as we shall see, identified with Indra. Similarly, the dragon-slaying deity with the 'vajra' is also called Indra, and the phallic Tree of Life is equally associated with the powerful soma-drinking Indra.

In the Avesta, the Lordship of the Abyss is represented by the fire-god in the extreme fiery form of **Xvarenah** (a name cognate with Varuna). In Mihr Yasht (X),127 Xvarenah is represented as going before Verethraghna (Vishnu),[32] who himself precedes Mithra – who heralds the sun, Hvare. Verethraghna himself is preceded by Atar, the Iranian counterpart of Agni. In Mihr Yasht (X),70, we find Verethraghna/ Vishnu, as Mithra's herald in the form of a boar (the original form of the wind Vāyu through which Vishnu first extracts Earth from the Abyss). In Mihr Yasht X,13, too, the sun Hvare follows Mithra. Thus we see that the order of the solar formation, **Xvarenah (Varuna), Verethraghna (Indra), Mithra, Hvare (Āditya/Nāsatyas)** is the same in the Avesta as in the Vedas. This order is, besides, a repetition in the underworld of the primal cosmic sequence – constituted of the fiery desire of Ātman (Agni), followed by Vāyu and the Cosmic Egg – that produced the Heavenly Light of Brahman (Āditya).

---

[32]   That Verethraghna corresponds to Vishnu is made clear by the fact that in the Verethraghna Yasht (14), 2, Vāyu is the first incarnation of Verethraghna (see above p.10n), Vāyu being the form that the deity assumes to operate on the waters (see above p.10).

Xvarenah becomes the force of the Lord of Earth. This is made clear by the fact that the Zamyad Yasht which is dedicated to the Lord of Earth, is actually addressed to Xvarenah. Xvarenah is, in Zamyad Yast (XIX),18, said to belong to all the Amesha (immortal) Spentas (blessed spirits) "who are the makers and governors, the shapers and overseers, the keepers and preservers of these creations of Ahura Mazda." Yima (called the ruler of the universe, the "sevenfold earth" in the same Yasht, 31,[33] succeeds for a while in retaining this xvarenah, but loses it once falsehood enters his mind, at which point the xvarenah flies out of him in the form of a falcon (wareghna), which also happens to be the seventh incarnation of Verethraghna (Bahram Yasht (XIV),19ff).[34] Yima's rulership over Earth suggests that he is ultimately the same as the First Man. Yima is also the ancestor of the present human race and is the counterpart of the seventh Manu of the Padmakalpa, Manu Vaivasvata, Manu of the Sun.[35] The falcon form of Verethraghna is clearly related to the sun, as the iconography of the Egyptian Horus demonstrates.

In its falcon form, Xvarenah first flies to Mithra (35), then to Thraetaona, and finally to

---

[33] The xvarenah is said to belong particularly to "the Aryan countries" (Yasht XIX,56).

[34] Of the ten incarnations of Verethraghna, the first is as Vāyu (the Wind), then as a bull, a horse, a camel, a boar, a youth, a falcon, a ram, a goat and, finally, a man. The falcon is a typical symbol of the sun of our system.

[35] The seventh Manu is a form of the first. That is why the name Ymir is used for the macroanthropos (the first Manu) in the Germanic Edda (see below p.54).

Keresaspa,[36] son of Thraetaona. We have seen above that Thraetaona battles the monster Asi Dahaka for the possession of this precious substance and that Thraetona must be closely related to Atar. In Zamyad Yasht XIX,51ff, Atar succeeds in restoring the Xvarenah to the Vouru-Kasha[37] sea.

The literal Roman counterpart to Varuna/Xvarenah is **Quirinus**, whose name is patently similar to the Iranian Xvarenah. Some scholars have suggested that Qurinus may be derived from an original form Co-Virīnus,[38] where Virinus, or Virinos, would be a derivative of 'vir' (man/Purusha), in which case the Greek Ouranos and Sanskrit Varuna may be related semantically to the Sanskritic Purusha rather than the Sanskritic Dyaus (shining Heaven), though both signify the same early cosmic phenomenon.

Among the Norsemen, the god called **Aegir** is possibly related phonetically and semantically to the Sumerian En-ki (Lord of Earth), who is the counterpart of the Indic Varuna. He is represented as a sea-god in 'Skaldasparmal' (*Prose Edda*), since Earth is surrounded by an Ocean (Okeanos)[39] and, in the 'Hymiskvida' (*Poetic Edda*), as a god who brews ale (the equivalent of the Indic 'soma') for the Aesir. In the 'Hymiskvida' Aegir complains that he does

---

[36] Keresaspa may be the Iranian original of the Sanskrit Kashyapa, whose consort is Aditi, mother of the sun, Āditya (see footnote above p.23n).

[37] The name Vouru-kasha is certainly related to the Sanskrit word for Tree, vrksha.

[38] See Jaan Puhvel, *Comparative Mythology*, Johns Hopkins University Press, 1987, p.150.

[39] Earth is the 'underworld' that is surrounded by an Ocean (Okeanos). Hence the Lord of Earth is also an Ocean-god.

not possess a cauldron (a phallic symbol) to brew ale for his guests in. Thor ventures to obtain such a cauldron from Hymir, a 'giant' who clearly represents the virility of Ymir/Purusha in the underworld. Aegir thus represents Enki/Varuna, the castrated primal Heaven that is sunk in the underworld (Earth), waiting to be revived by the storm-god.

The Nordic counterpart of the god of fire itself, Agni, is **Loki**, who features prominently in the Eddic poem 'Lokasena,' which begins with a narration of Aegir's feast.

II. i

INDRA-VERETHRAGHNA-THOR

The second birth of Agni is from the Earth. In *SB* VI,7,4,3 the second birth is said to be one effected by the brāhman priests themselves since they officiate as Maitrāvaruna priests representing the lords of Earth:

> 'from **us** [the Mitra-Varuna brāhman priests] the second time, the knower of beings,' — inasmuch as he, man-like, on that occasion generated him a second time;

Similarly, in *Krishna Yajur Veda* IV,2,2, the second birth of Agni is described as equivalent to that which occurs in the kindling of the sacred fire by the brāhman priests:

> From **us** secondly [was born] he who knoweth all.[40]

The Battle Against the Serpent Vrtra

The rise of the solar force in the underworld into the Mid-region of our universe as the sun is not possible

---

[40]   i.e., Agni Jātavedas.

until the serpent at the foot of the Tree, in the depths of the Ocean, is destroyed. This serpent, which represents the force of Earthly constraint, is destroyed not by the solar god himself, since he is at first moribund in the underworld (as Varuna) and then puerile, as the incipient sun (Mitra), but rather by the storm-god (Teshup, Zeus) who was initially the adversary of his solar counterpart, Brahman/Ouranos. The vital force which fells the fiery sky or solar force and causes the latter to descend into the "underworld" is, thus, not an entirely inimical one since it is the same that will destroy the serpent, separate the earth from heaven in our universe and allow, first, the moon and, then, the sun to rise to the Mid-region of the stars.

The serpent at the base of the cosmic tree holds the seed (Soma) that will reinvigorate the castrated Heaven in the underworld so that his phallus can rise as the universe in the form of a Tree of Life in the Mid-Region between Earth and Heaven. In *BP* V,25,1, the serpent **Sesha,** on whom the fallen Heaven reposes, is described as being the tāmasic or Māya-associated aspect of the supreme lord, which sustains this universe by the magical effect of sympathy. In the Eddas too, the Midgard serpent is represented as encircling the earth.[41]

In the Indian system of Kundalini Yoga, the **Kundalini serpent** (which is analogous to Vrtra)[42] is represented in the microcosm as the force of vitality as well as sexuality coiled at the base of the spinal

---

[41]   *The Prose Edda*, Ch.47; cf. 'Gylfaginning.'

[42]   See V.G. Rele, V.G. Rele, *The Vedic Gods as Figures of Biology*, Bombay: D.B. Taraporevala Sons, 1931, p.104.

cord.[43] The aim of the yogic discipline is, as Cook puts it,

> to awaken this sleeping force and get it to climb the spinal tree, piercing the various spiritual centres (chakras) along its way, until finally it is released [like Brahman from atop the petals of the lotus in the Puranas or the sun from atop the sycamore in Egypt] from the Sahasra Chakra, the Thousand-petalled Lotus, at the top of the head. At this point the heavy material forces of the earth and the waters, ... take flight... The mythical eagle Garuda[44] carries off Kundalini in its beak; heaven and earth, light and darkness, spirit and flesh are finally, ecstatically united.[45]

The sublimation of the serpentine force marks the rise of the soul, Ātman, to its original brilliance as the divine Consciousness, Brahman.

---

[43] See R. Cook. *op.cit.*, p.25. The fact that the serpent provides Adam and Eve with sexual awareness in Genesis reveals the ultimate reliance of the Hebrew Bible on Indo-European sources, even though the spiritual significance of the story of the cosmic man is entirely ignored by the priestly redactors of the Bible.

[44] Garuda is an early unruly form of the sun that must also, like the Phoenix, be controlled before our sun can emerge in the heavens.

[45] See R. Cook, *ibid.* That this process is akin to a sexual orgasm is not surprising considering the significance of the phallus even in the macrocosmic creation. The "flood" which accompanies the emergence of the sun in our universe (see below p.39) is thus naturally related to the waves of pleasure that suffuse one's mind in sexual ecstasy.

In the Vedas, **Vrtra** is a serpentine cosmic phenomenon represented as being located within a turbulent wind. Vrtra is a demon of resistance that prevents the "mountain" from ejecting its life-giving seed. That Vrtra hides the fiery Agni within itself is confirmed by *AV* III,21,1 where there is particular reference to the form of Agni within Vrtra along with those within the waters, man, stones, herbs, and forest trees.[46] *KYV* II,5,2, Vrtra is said to be called Vrtra because "he enveloped these worlds."[47] In *TS* II,iv,12,2, Vrtra is said to have grown and enveloped the three worlds.[48]

Indra is the hero chosen by the gods to defeat the dragon, Vrtra, when all of the Ādityas, Vāsus, Rudras, and gods were paralysed by the monster (*RV* 10,48,11). Indeed, Indra's freeing of the waters from the restriction imposed on them by the dragon Vrtra is associated with the creation of our heaven and earth, which are formed out of Vrtra's body (*RV* I,36,8).

In *BP* VI,9,18, Vrtra is said to cover the universe in darkness, which is not surprising considering that his father Tvashtr is the same as the Greek Tartarus, who, according to Hesiod (*Theogony*, 820-22), is the parent of Typhon. And, as Plutarch noted of the Greek hydra, "**Typhon** is the element of the soul

---

[46] We will remember that Loki, in the Norse mythology, is the father of the serpent Jörmungandr.

[47] The etymology of the word, however, is more accurately preserved in the Avestan "Vrθra" meaning "resistance" (see A.K. Lahiri, *Vedic Vrtra*, Delhi: Motilal Banarsidass, 1984, p.73).

[48] It is in order to combat this control of the three worlds by Vrtra that Vishnu expands through these worlds with his three gigantic steps (see below) and thus allows Indra to hurl his thunderbolt against the monster (see A.K. Lahiri, *op.cit.*, p.195).

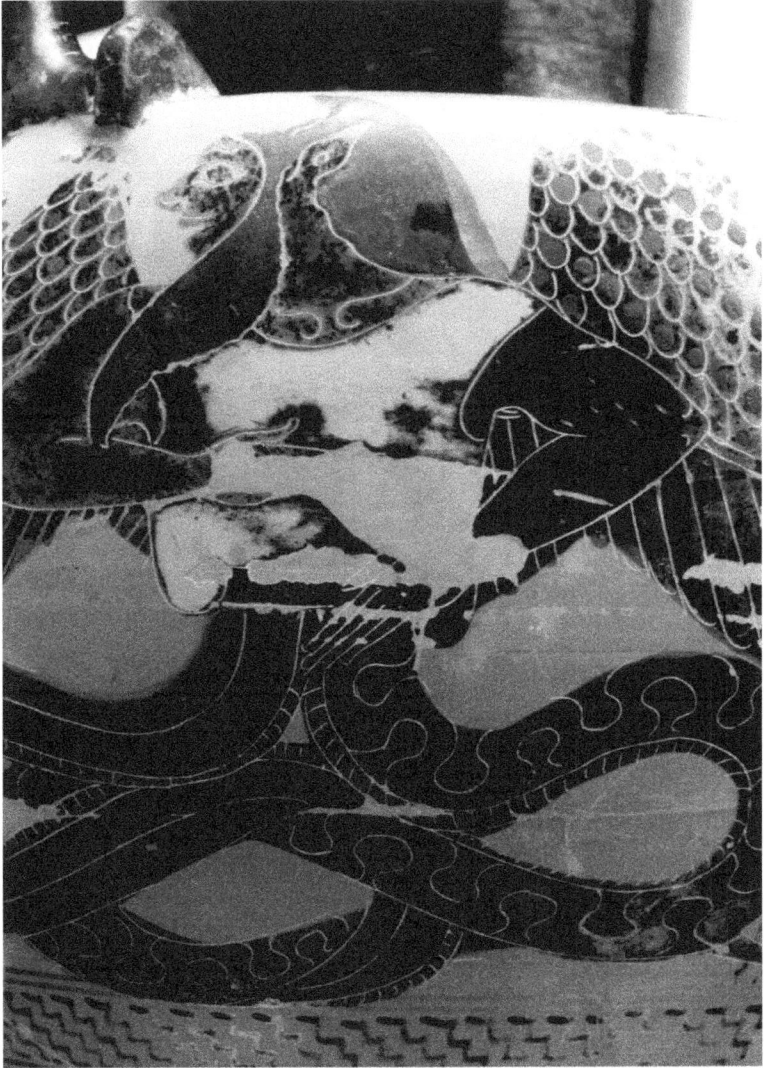

Fig. 5 - Typhon, Greek jar, 6ᵗʰ c. B.C.

which is passionate, akin to the Titans, without reason, and brutish, and the element of the corporeal which is subject to death, disease and confusion."[49]

In *RV* V,40,5, there is a reference to Indra's dispelling of the magical spell of the Asura "Svarbhānu" which surrounded the sun with darkness. These passages thus seem to refer to the liberation of the solar energy from its original concealment in gaseous matter. Indra is also associated with the discovery of the "lights" for the benefit of living creatures and men in particular (*RV* VIII,15,5). *RV* III,39,6 further states that Indra "took the light, discerning it from darkness." Indra is said to have discovered Agni among the waters.

Vrtra is indeed an Asuric creation of Tvashtr (just as Typhon is a child of Tartarus) who developed this monster of resistance when Indra felled his first offspring, **Vishvarūpa** (*RV* II,11,19), who is represented as a "three-headed" monster. Vishvarūpa is perhaps the counterpart of the Iranian **Asi Dahaka.**

Indra also succeeds in freeing the "cows" from the "vala," a rocky enclosure in which they are hidden by the evil **Panis.** The "cows" in the vala myth (10.67,1-12) symbolise the radiant solar energy, since *RV* I,164,3 suggests that this is the secret name of the rays of the dawn. In *RV* X, 108, 5, the "cows" are described as "flying around to the ends of the sky." The Panis themselves are described in *BP* V,24,30 as serpentine, Asuric creations of Diti and Danu and inhabit Rasātala, the sixth of the seven subterranean regions of the material universe bordering on the last, called Pātāla, below which lies the serpent Sesha. The Panis are thus related to Sesha/Vrtra and are

---

49 Plutarch, *De Iside et Osiride*, p.197.

particularly associated with the primordial frigidity that obstructs the emergence of the solar rays in our system. "Vala," significantly, is the same term that is used in the Avesta ("vara") for the ark that bears Yima during the flood that accompanies the birth of the sun. This ark is representative of the life of our universe in the Mid-region.[50]

It is apparent thus that the separation of primal Heaven from Earth by Kāla/Chronos is repeated in the underworld ("earth") by Indra in order to allow the rise of the solar energy from there into the Mid-region of the stars. In *RV* VII, 23,3, it is stated that "Indra when he had slain resistless foemen, forced with his might the two world-halves asunder." In *RV* VI,8, this act of separation of heaven from earth, normally attributed to Indra, is ascribed also to Mitra, since Mitra is the early form of Indra as the sun:[51] "Wonderful Mitra propped the heaven and earth apart, … He made the two bowls [i.e., earth and heaven] part asunder like two skins."

Indra's destruction of Vrtra, the second "monster" created by Tvashtr, is celebrated with equal fervour by the Zoroastrians as an achievement not of Indra himself but, rather, of **Verethraghna** (Destroyer of Vrtra), who corresponds to Indra's solar form, **Vishnu.** We may assume that Verethra

---

[50] The Vedic vala myth is thus a cosmological archetype of the Flood story. The animals saved from the deluge in the later Sumerian and Indo-Iranian Flood stories, as well as in the account of Noah in the Hebrew Bible derived from them, are – unlike the elements of solar energy symbolically referred to in *RV* as "cows" – real animals, and therefore associated with the seeds of all animal life borne by the Vedic Cow [Earth], as well as by the Iranian Bull.

[51] See below p.57.

is the "**lizard**" at the base of the Vouru-kasha sea, the Iranian equivalent of the Abyss. In the Tir Yasht devoted to the god Tisthrya, the release of the waters is due to the destruction of **Apaosha** (Yasht VIII,29)[52] as well as of the **Pairikas** (Yasht VIII, 40) (evil spirits that may correspond to the Panis of the Vedas).

In the Germanic Eddas, the god who battles the serpent-like Seth and Zeus is **Thor**, who is called "son of earth [that is, the Lord of Earth/Enki/Varuna]" in the Eddic 'Lokasena,' 58. We have noted that it is Thor who obtains the 'cauldron' that the ailing Aegir lacks to brew ale (soma) in. In the *Prose Edda* 'Gylfaginning,' ch.48, Thor battles a dragon, the **Midgard serpent**. Thor thus has to battle the serpent of 'tāmasic' power (or 'inertia') at the base of the Tree in the underworld (Earth) before he can rise through the Tree as the sun. That is why he is typically represented as wielding a hammer, Mjölnir. In the 'Hymiskvida' from the *Poetic Edda*, Thor kills the Midgard serpent **Jörmungandr**,[53] (who is engendered by Loki)[54] while on a boat with Hymir, who owns the cauldron that Aegir needs to brew ale in. The Midgard serpent is, in the end, consigned to the Ocean around Earth, which it then encircles.[55]

---

[52] A name which may be related to the Egyptian serpent Apop.

[53] In the 'Skáldskaparmál' of the *Prose Edda,* Sturluson mentions Nidhogg and Jormungand as two of the several names of the serpent. *Nid* (Old Norse *níð)* is related to Old High Germanic *nidding* and modern German *Neid,* meaning envy and malice.

[54] See 'Gylfaginning' Ch.34, in the *Prose Edda.*

[55] See 'Gylfaginning,' Ch.48.

Fig. 6 - Thor and Jörmungandr,
Lorenz Frølich (1820-1908).

Soma

The revival of the potency of Dyaus is accomplished by Indra through the imbibing of **Soma**, the essence of life and immortality that is represented as ale in Germanic mythology, and wine in the Dionysiac.

It is interesting to note that, in the *Skanda Purāna,* the fig tree (which symbolises the life of the emergent universe as the phallic Tree of Life) at the centre of the cosmic streams is said to be unshaken by the "doomsday hurricane."[56] In the Nordic Edda too, the Yggdrasil which is destroyed at Ragnarök will inevitably revive the creation after this destruction since it contains within its trunk all the seeds of life.[57] This plenitude of life within the tree is also symbolised by the Moon, which bears the **seeds** of universal animal life, according to the *Bundahishn.*[58]

We may compare this to the Vedic hymn to Soma (also called Indu, the moon) who represents the life-force or seed stored in the moon as well as the vital substance of the light:

> These rapid Soma-streams have stirred themselves to motion like strong steeds,
>
> ....
>
> Immortal, cleansed, these drops, since first they flowed, have never wearied,
> fain
> To reach the regions and their paths.
> Advancing they have travelled o'er the ridges

---

[56] See S. Shastri, *op.cit.,* p.65.

[57] See "Voluspa"; cf. R. Cook, *The Tree of Life: Symbol of the Centre,* London: Thames and Hudson, 1974, p.12.

[58] See below p.41.

of the earth and heaven,
And this the highest realm of all (*RV* IX, 22)

and

Swift Soma drops have been effused in streams
of meath, the gladdening drink,
For sacred lore of every kin.
Hither to newer resting-place the ancient
Living Ones [Soma drops] are come.
They made the Sun that he might shine. (23)

The animal life of the universe, as we note from
the Iranian evidence below, is stored in the moon.
According to *RV* IX,42,1, Soma is considered as the
progenitor of the sun. The moon itself is said to be
formed by the infusion of Soma into the waters (*SB*
IV,vi,7,12). Soma then engenders the sun in floods
along with the other stars. Soma here is clearly
identical to Indra filled with Soma. Indeed, in *RV*
IX,5, Soma is hymned as the bull and the "self" of
Indra himself.

Indra is always closely associated with the "Soma"
or seminal fluid of the universe, and he is called the
"lord of the seed."[59] Indra is said to have imbibed the
sap of life, Soma (seed), in the dwelling of Tvashtr,
who is an aspect of Dyaus. Soma is described in *RV*
III,48,2-3 as that milk which Indra's mother, Aditi,
"poured for thee [Indra] in thy mighty Father's
dwelling./ Desiring food he came unto his Mother,

---

[59]   *Mahābhārata* I, 57, 1-27.

and on her breast beheld the pungent Soma."[60] In *RV* III,I,7, the infant "Agni" is said to be nourished by the "milch-kine" (solar rays), which are present in the seven cosmic rivers that issue out of the mountain when Indra destroys the serpent Vrtra. The "cows" (the water of Aditi) are said to be impregnated by the "bull."

In *RV* I,84,15 the "milch-kine" are said to have recognized their lord as Tvashtr's Bull in the mansion of the **moon**, the moon being the heavenly body in which the Soma will be finally stored. Soma thus represents the creative potency of fire, which is responsible for the formation of our universe and its light but must nevertheless be controlled in order to allow the sun to emerge as the ruler of the universe. The moon, which is associated with Soma, is indeed considered to be a form of Agni as Kāma (Desire). The moon and Soma are also often identified with Vrtra, who contains the soma.[61] Soma, symbolising the moon, is also said to be the "food" of the sun (also a form of Indra) (*SB* I,vi,4,18), since the sun "consumes" its soma.

It will be apparent that Indra's intoxication with Soma is clearly the source of the Thracian Dionysiac and Bacchic wine-rituals.

Exactly as in the Iranian sacred literature,[62] **the pressing of Soma** is considered as a sacrifice of the god Soma. Soma is identified with the primal

---

[60] That soma is ultimately the same as (Ger.) samen/seed, which infuses Indra as the "Tree" of Life, is clear from this reference to Indra consuming soma at his mother's breast, since, according to the *Bundahishn* Ch.XVI,5, the woman's milk is produced by the male seed just as blood is produced by the female.

[61] See A.K. Lahiri, *op.cit.*, pp.172-87.

[62] See below p.42.

Prajāpati himself (or more precisely, his semen) in *Shatapatha Brāhmana* III,9,4,17, since, as we have seen, the latter's sacrifice is essentially a castration of his seed-filled phallus, and the seed of Prajāpati, Soma, is what supplies the universe with life. Soma is commonly understood to be an aphrodisiac pressed from the soma plant and consumed by the Āryan priests during the ritual.[63] The Scythians, as we have noted, are indeed called "haomavarga Sakas," or soma-drinking Scythians,[64] and archaeological finds at the BMAC in Afghanistan include vessels stained with plant-juice. But the real significance of Soma in the Āryan literature is as the life-force of the macroanthropos. Indra's establishment of the solar force in the heavens is due to the potency derived from the Soma within him.

In the Iranian *Bundahishn*, the seed of the Bull (representing all animal life)[65] slaughtered by Angra Mainyu is purified and stored in the moon,[66] just as the seed of the slaughtered First Man (representing

---

[63] The Vedic sacrifice involving the extraction of soma is called "kratu," while that without it is a "yajna."

[64] So in the inscriptions of Darius I (see P.O. Skjaervo, "The Avesta as source for the early history of the Iranians," in G. Erdosy, (ed.) *The Indo-Aryans of Ancient South Asia*, Berlin: Walter de Gruyter, 1995, p.157). Herodotus (VII,64) mentions that Saka was the name given by the Persians to the Scythians. The Behistun inscription (ca.522-486 B.C.) of Darius the Great refers to the Sakas in its Babylonian section as "Gimmirai" (Cimmerians), showing that they were closely related to the Celts in spite of the fact that the latter were western, centum-speaking Āryans.

[65] The seed of the dead Bull stored in the moon is the same as the life of the universe preserved after the "deluge" by the first man, Yima/Ziusudra/Manu.

[66] See *Bundahishn* X, 1-2; cf. *Fargard* XXI,9 and *Sirozah* I,12.

all human life) is stored in the sun.[67] The Bull is thus, in the *Greater Bundahishn*,[68] likened to the shining Moon. Similarly, the First Man is likened to the shining sun (where his seed will be purified). In the Haoma-sacrifice, **Hoama** is represented anthropomorphically, for the pressing of the soma plant in this sacrifice is represented as a slaying of a primal god, Haoma or his anthropomorphic form **Duroasha** (or Frashmi), in order to extract his productive essence.[69] Duraosha is said to have been in existence even before Vivanghvant, the solar father of Yima (Manu Vaivasvata).[70] Yima is said to be the one who corrupted the Haoma rite by burning the sacred plant (Yasna XXXII,8). Haoma is declared to have been prepared for the corporeal world first by Vivanghavant (the sun) (Hom Yast IX, 3), and fourthly by Pourushaspa, father of Zarathustra. Duraosha is sacrificed so that the vital force of Haoma may be expressed in the world. In the haoma-sacrifice, therefore, the pressing of the soma plant thus symbolises the extraction of the life-force of Haoma/Soma.

Haoma is considered by the Zoroastrians to be not only a source of immortality but also a destroyer of the Daevas (I,6). Ironically, in the Vedas, it is Indra, the chief of the Devas, who kills Vrtra.

---

[67]   *Bundahishn* XV.

[68]   See R.C. Zaehner, *The Teachings of the Magi*, London: George Allen and Unwin Ltd., 1956, p.40.

[69]   See E.O. James, *The Tree of Life: An Archaeological Study*, Leiden: E.J. Brill, 1966, p.26.

[70]   Yasna IX,17,27; X, 21; XLIII,5.

II. ii
INDRA-FREYR

Ashvattha - the Tree of Life

We know that the divine phallus was absorbed by Zeus/Teshup so that the entire universe moved into his "stomach." The rising phallic force of this deity in the underworld is often represented as a "tree" of life. The universal tree has its roots in the Abyss, while its trunk represents Earth and branches in the Mid-region. Atop its branches, in Heaven, will emerge the full-fledged sun.

In the Indic sacred literature, the 'ashvattha' fig-tree is considered to be inverted, so that its roots grow upwards and its branches spread downwards.[71] The fact that the tree is an analogue of the phallus is made clear by the reference in *Linga Purāna* 17ff. Also, the phallus is an endless column of fire that fills the universe, and at the top of which is Brahma in the solar form of a swan (hamsa) and at the base of which is Vishnu in the form of a boar.[72] The sun-god (Sūrya/Āditya) is a later manifestation within our universe of the original light of the universe, Brahman, which appeared above the "lotus" Earth.

The tree of life spans the entire universe, comprising the three regions of earth, the mid-region, and the heavens, which are dominated respectively by the three forms that the solar energy assumes in our universe as well as in the primal

---

[71]   *Katha Upanishad*, VI,1.

[72]   The representation of Vishnu as a boar corresponds to that of Vāyu in the primal cosmos. The boar form of Verethreghna also heralds Mithra in the Avesta, Mihir Yasht XVIII.

cosmos – Agni, Vāyu, Āditya. Agni is, in *KYV* V,5,1, called "the lowest of deities,"[73] while Vishnu (i.e., as Āditya) is the highest. In the *Maitrāyana Upanishad* VI,4, the tree (called metonymously "Brahman") is called "three-footed", and from the evidence of the Germanic Edda we may consider these feet or roots as not restricted to heaven but as equally embracing Heaven, Earth, and the Mid-Region.

Varuna, in *RV* I,24,7, "sustaineth erect the Tree's stem in the baseless region [the Abyss, apsu]," for Varuna is the Lord of the Abyss. The roots of the tree arise from deep within the Abyss, while the trunk represents Earth. The branches of the Tree of Life represent the Mid-region of the manifest universe and the sun, which arises from atop them, rules the heavens. The *Maitrāyana Upanishad* passage mentioned above further makes clear that the "branches," which represent the Mid-region of the manifest universe, contain "space, wind, fire, water, earth and the like." The summit of the tree, that is, the highest point of its branches, represents Heaven, the domain of the gods. The highest of the three heavens serves as the seat of the gods (*AV* V,4,3,4). There the Ādityas (suns) enjoy their nectar of immortality, while Yama (*RV* X,135,1) is ruler of the lowest heaven.

In the *Mahābhārata*, the infant Vishnu is found under an "ashvattha" tree during the flood, which may be a depiction of the sun of the underworld since the roots of the tree are in the Abyss. The use of **Vishnu** as the deity at the base of the phallus [tree] in the *Linga Purāna* is related to the evolution of the solar force from the moribund Varuna. In the Avesta,

---

[73] The first of the Ādityas, Mitra-Varuna, are the lords of rta, the justice interwoven into the fabric of the universe.

interestingly, Vishnu (Verethraghna) is represented as a boar, which is the form associated with Vāyu.[74] In fact, the Tree is the locus of the second universal form of Agni arisen from Earth[75] and one displaying the power of Vāyu/Wotan, the Wind-god.[76]

Vishnu is extolled in *RV* VII,99,3 as a companion of Indra's in the task of the separation of Heaven and Earth, though it may be that Vishnu's particular competence is in keeping these two realms apart. Vishnu represents the expansive and sustaining form of Agni, much like Vāyu. In *RV* VII,99, Vishnu is said to firmly support the two halves of the universe, heaven and earth, while he holds fast earth among the waters (Okeanos) which surround it by fixing it with "pegs." According to *SB* XI,viii,1, the "pegs" are "mountains" and "rivers": "He sets this [earth] firmly with the help of mountains and rivers." These mountains and rivers may not be terrestrial, since the source from which the material universe, as well as its light, arises is itself Earth in the form of a mountain, while the rivers may be the seven streams flowing through the universe. The universe is said to have been spread out through Vishnu's sacrificial fervour. It is, thus, spiritual intensity that apparently causes the spatial expansion of our universe.

In *RV* V,85, the separation of the heavens from the earth normally attributed to Indra/Vishnu is identified with **Varuna** himself, who is said to have spread forth the earthly element "as a skin to spread in front of Surya" and "standing in the firmament hath meted the earth out with the sun as with a

---

[74] See above p.10.

[75] See above p.29.

[76] Cf. the association of Wotan with the Yggdrasil tree below.

measure." In *KYV* I, 2, 14, Varuna is also called the bull that "hath stablished the sky, the atmosphere/ Hath meted the breadth of the earth" (I, 2,8), for "All these are Varuna's ordinances."

The tree of life holds Heaven and Earth together and is also identified with **Indra**. Indra is called "the Bull" who has drunk the powerful Soma:

> 6. This Bull's most gracious far-extended favour existed first of all in full abundance.

> By his support they [the Ādityas] are maintained in common who in the Asura's mansions dwell together.

> 7. What was the tree, what wood,[77] in sooth, produced it, from which they fashioned forth the Earth and Heaven?

> These Twain [earth and heaven] stand fast and wax not old for ever: …

> … He is the Bull, the Heaven's and Earth's supporter.

In *AV* IV,11,2 Indra is called the "draft ox" who sustains the earth and heaven.

In *RV* III,31, Indra develops into a universal tree as a result of his consumption of soma, and this soma-inspired growth holds Earth and Heaven together:

---

[77] This particular curiosity with regard to the "wood" of the tree clearly refers to the nature of the erect phallus.

11. For [Indra] the Cow [Aditi], noble and far-extending, poured pleasant juices, bringing oil and sweetness.

12. They [the kine] made a mansion for their Father [their protector, Indra], deftly provided him a great and glorious dwelling/ With firm support parted and stayed the Parents [Heaven and Earth], and sitting, fixed him there erected, mighty.

13. What time the ample chalice [of soma] had impelled him, swift waxing, vast, to pierce the earth and heaven.

and *RV* II,15:

High heaven unsupported in space he stablished: he filled the two worlds [earth and heaven] and the air's Mid-region.

Earth he upheld, and gave it wide expansion. These things did Indra in the Soma's rapture.

It has been suggested, also, that, in the human microcosmos, the Tree may be manifest as the central nervous system.[78] Since the base of the spinal cord is the seat of unconscious, as well as of sexual, activity, it is indeed the task of spiritual man in the yogic system to rise to supraconsciousness by mastering the "serpent." The tree that sustains the microcosmos as well as the macrocosmos is, indeed, filled with the

---

[78] For an understanding of the tree within the human microcosm as the structure of the entire nervous system itself, see V.G. Rele, *op.cit.*, pp.26f.

seed of desire which, when it succeeds in producing the clear light of consciousness (Brahman) in enlightened man, at once prompts the destruction of the tree itself as an illusion.[79]

According to the Iranian *Greater Bundahishn*, Ch.XIV, the First Man, Gayomard gave birth autoerotically to the twins Mashye and Mashyane, who grew up "in the semblance of a **tree**, whose fruit was the ten races of mankind" (10). We have seen that the Tree of Life represents the life of the universe in the Mid-Region between Earth and Heaven. Gayomard is the same as Brahman/Prajāpati/Ouranos, who is struck down by Chronos and his son Ganesha/Zeus/Seth and forced into the underworld.

In the Avesta (Rashn Yasht, XII,17), it is stated that, in the centre of the Vouru-kasha Sea (the Abyss), stands "the **tree of the eagle** ... that is called the tree of good remedies ... on which rest the seeds of all plants." At the base of the tree is a "lizard" created by Ahriman to destroy the tree. However, ten fish save the tree by continually swimming around it.[80]

As regards the "sun-bird" or "eagle" that also appears in the fire-altars of the Vedic Indians, we note, on the Indic Mitanni seals of the second millennium B.C., that the winged disk representing the emergence of the sun[81] is sometimes supported on a sacred pillar, while on other seals the wings of the disk are transformed into the branches of a tree.

---

[79]　This characteristic Indo-European spirituality is recovered in the West in the philosophy of Arthur Schopenhauer (especially in his *Die Welt als Wille und Vorstellung*, 1819).

[80]　See *Bundahishn*, XVIII,2.

[81]　The wings are those of a falcon, which, in Egyptian as well as Avestan religion, represents a solar form of the divine energy.

The branches of the Tree of Life, as we have seen, represent the Mid-Region between heaven and earth, and the bird itself must represent the eagle of the Avesta.

In the poetic Edda, the name of the **Yggdrasil** ash-tree may be phonetically related to the Vedic Indra.[82] We may note the similarity of the description of this tree in "Voluspa" and "Grimnismal" to those in the Vedas, as well as in Near Eastern cosmological literature:

> I know an ash-tree stands called Yggdrasill,
> a high tree, soaked with shining loam.[83]

and:

> Three roots there grow in three directions
> under the ash of Yggdrasil;

---

[82] 'Yggdra' is pronounced 'Indra'. The use of a suffix 'šiel' is noticeable in the Indic divine names mentioned in the Mitanni treaty. The popular interpretation of Yggdrasil, however (see, for instance, R. Cook, *op.cit.*, p.23), is as "steed of Odin", from Ygg, one of the names of this god meaning "the terrible" (see 'Grimnismal', st.54). The tree is associated with the horse in the Odin myth as well as in shamanistic rituals which depict the "ride" or "ascent" of the shaman to heaven (see M. Eliade, *Shamanism,* p.270). Indeed, the Vedic term "ashvattha" for the fig-tree itself contains the word for horse "ashva". The conflation of arboreal and equestrian symbolism is perhaps related to the original conception of the universe as a phallus and of the sun that illuminates it. In the royal horse-sacrifice of the Indo-Āryans, the horse is said to be produced from the "left eye" of Prajāpati (*SB* XIII,iii,1,1) so that the sacrifice of the horse is meant to restore this eye to its proper place. The eye is here clearly a symbol of the sun.

[83] Voluspa, 19, in *Poetic Edda*, p.6. The "shining loam" is the same as "soma", the life-giving sap of the cosmic tree.

> Hel lives under one, under the second the
> frost-giants,
> the third humankind.
> Ratatosk is the squirrel's name who has to run
> upon the ash of Yggdrasil;
> the eagle's[84] word he must bring from above
> and tell to Nidhogg below.[85]

Like the Indian tree, the Yggdrasil also grows downwards, since one of its roots is said to be based in the heavens, where the primal gods (Aesir/Asuras) hold court. Under this root is the well of Urd.[86] In one region of heaven called Valaskjalf (the hall of the slain) is to be found the seat of Odin, called Hlidskjalf, whence he surveys the nine worlds covered by the tree [there being three heavens, as well as three mid-regions and earths].

The second root reaches the Ginnungagap (the Abyss), where the "frost ogres" dwell. An oracular spring guarded by the sage Mimir is to be found here. This region represents the waters from which the sun is finally born (just as it is born also from Heaven and from Earth). The third root ends in Hel, or Niflheim, which is Earth as well as the land of the dead, the underworld. At the base of this region dwells the serpent Nidhogg[87] in the well called Hvergelmir.

We may assume that between Niflheim and Heaven is the realm of Ymir, which is the Mid-region of the material universe. In Indic literature, the lower

---

[84] The eagle represents the sun.

[85] 'Grimnismal,' 31-32, in *Poetic Edda*.

[86] 'Gylfaginning' in *Prose Edda*.

[87] The name "Nidhogg" means "striker that destroys" (cf. *Prose Edda*, p.43).

heavens is ruled by Yama, who is also the king of the dead. The "squirrel" which bears the "word" of the eagle in the branches of the cosmic ash to the serpent below must represent the jīva (life-force) as described in the *Dhyānabindhu Upanishad* and the Kundalini-Yoga system. That the Nordic tree represents the axis from which the sun is born is made clear in the verses that refer to "Arvak and Alsvid," two horses that "must pull wearily the sun from here."[88]

If Thor represents the dragon-slaying Indra in the Germanic mythology, the reviving phallic power of Indra is represented there by the ithyphallic god, **Freyr**. In Adam of Bremen's *Gesta Hammaburgensis* (11th century) we note the worship of three major deities in the Temple of Uppsala, Thor flanked by Woden and Frikko (Freyr). Thor, as we have seen, is the martial aspect of the storm-god Zeus/Ganesha/Indra. Frikko/Freyr as an ithyphallic deity corresponds to the Indra/Ganesha/Zeus/Dionysus that has imbibed the soma, the erotic or desire-filled force that revives the moribund Ouranos/Dyaus in the underworld, Earth. Wotan/Vāyu is the extending force that maintains the erection of the phallus of the sunken Purusha as the Tree of Life through which the sun rises to the heavens.

---

[88] 'Grimnismal,' 37. These horses may be the Germanic counterparts of the Indic Nāsatyas. The name of the shield of the sun, "Svalin," in 'Grimnismal,' 38, may be derived from the same root ("svar"=to shine) which gave Suwalliyat/Sūrya.

Fig. 7 - Freyr, statuette, Viking age.

II. iii

WOTAN-VĀYU

The Sacrifice of the Tree

The solar force, which has been forced into the underworld by the storm-force, has now to be gradually cleansed of its material elements. This purification, which allows the sun to acquire its tremendous power in our universe is inextricably allied to the more general *contemptus mundi* and asceticism which underlie the theology of the solar religions, especially the Indic and the Dionysian-Orphic, as well as the Pythagorean-Platonic.[89]

We have seen that the Tree of Life may represent both the infrastructure of the material universe and the internal nervous structure and erotic energy of microcosmic man. The material universe being considered a result of the illusion of the divine Māya and incomparably inferior to the original Cosmic Light and Intellect; it is the duty of the yogi to detach himself from it by "cutting down" the Tree of Life. The Tree is itself thus represented as being cut down, or displaced, in some of the legends of the mythologies under consideration. Since the "tree" is an analogue for the divine phallus itself and its seminal power, Soma, the exhortation to cut it down in these mythic

---

[89]   For the Orphic religion see W.K.C. Guthrie, *Orpheus and Greek Religion*, p.156f. It is interesting to note that according to Hecateus of Abdera Orpheus introduced the mysteries of Dionysus and Demeter into Greece which were modelled on those of Osiris and Isis in Egypt (see M.L. West, *The Orphic Poems*, Oxford: Clarendon Press, 1983, p.26). For the Pythagorean doctrines see J.A. Philip, *Pythagoras*, p.137f.

accounts is clearly one to asceticism as well. The serpent at the bottom of the Abyss from whence the tree emerges is identifiable with the Māyā of the supreme deity as well as – microcosmically – with the Kundalini serpent at the base of the spinal cord. The injunction to cut down the tree, therefore, signifies the severing of the illusion of Egoity, which lies at the base of the axis of the universe through a mastery of the sexual force (Kāma, Desire) that is represented by the Kundalini serpent.

In the *Shiva Purāna* I,1,21,82-99, Kāma, who is Shiva's own erotic aspect and burnt down by **Shiva** in the form of a tree, is called the "evil at the root of all misery."[90] Here, the contest is plainly between the ascetic Shiva and the erotic passion that engenders and sustains the illusion of the universe.

In the *Mahābhārata (Bhagavad Gita)*, too, Krishna counsels Arjuna to cut down the ashvattha tree since the tree represents the world of sense-experience, *samsara*.[91]

In Germanic mythology the tree serves as the locus of the great **self-sacrifice** of the god Odin/**Wotan**/Wata to himself, which may be a repetition of the original killing of Ymir, the First Man:[92]

> I know that I hung on a windy tree
> nine long nights,
> wounded with a spear, dedicated to Odin,
> myself to myself.[93]

---

[90] See W.D. O'Flaherty, *Asceticism and Eroticism in the Mythology of Śiva*, London: Oxford University Press, 1973, p.159.

[91] See E.O. James, *op.cit.*, p.257.

[92] See below p.72.

[93] 'Havamal,' 138.

Fig. 8 - Odin on Yggdrasil, Lorenz Frølich (1820-1908).

This episode is similar to Shiva's burning of his erotic aspect Kāma in the form of a tree.[94] The reference to the "windy" tree is clearly related to Wotan's own nature as wind-god (Vāyu/Wata). It is as a result of this sacrifice – akin to the ordeals of Marduk and Tammuz and even the Christ[95] – that Odin achieves mastery of the magical runes, which provide insight into the inner workings of the universe and of Fate.

---

[94] See above p.54.

[95] The sacrifice preceding the birth of the sun is certainly related to the passion of the Christ on the Cross. The identification of the Christ with Apollo that we witness in early Christian art, for example, in the pre-Constantinian necropolis under St. Peter's basilica, was possible because of the original solar significance of the Christ story (see, in this context, T. Harpur, *Pagan Christ: Recovering the Lost Light*, Toronto: Thomas Allen, 2004).

II. iv
MITRA-MITHRA

The Emerging Sun

The Vedic god **Mitra** is the same as the earliest form of the emerging sun. The dual nature of Mitra-Varuna expressed in *RV* V,3,1: "Thou at thy birth art Varuna, O Agni; when thou art kindled thou becomest Mitra." Varuna and Mitra are said to be the quiescent and enflamed states of Agni.[96] Mitra is, on one occasion (*RV* VIII,25,4,), called a Deva (god), whereas his counterpart, Varuna, is in the same passage called an Asura, since the latter is a primal deity sunk in the underworld, or Earth.

In the Avesta, we have seen that Verethraghna is a herald of Mithra. So Vrtrahan (an epithet of Indra (RV VI,60,3)) must be a figure that heralds Mithra, who is the early form of the sun emergent from the dormant Varuna.

According to the Avestan Mihir Yasht, the sun Hvare (Sūrya) arises from the Hara mountain (Mihr Yasht, X,13), preceded by **Mithra**. Mithra is a son of Ahura, and, like the Vedic Mitra, is a priestly (brāhmanical) god (89). At 127 Mithra is described as being accompanied by Atar (Agni) "all in a blaze" and the "awful king Glory" [Xvarenah-Varuna]. Mithra, who heralds Hvare [Sūrya/Indra], is himself preceded by Verethraghna and Xvarenah (Varuna), who together represent the different stages of the sun noted above.

---

[96]   Cf. *RV* VII,88,2: "And now as I am come before his presence, I take the face of Varuna for Agni's."

Mithra is often adored in the form of a bull (86) and is said to be "the lord of wide pastures," which is clearly a reference to the wide-ranging extent of his course as a "bull." We know that Vishnu is also often admired for his wide strides (RV I,154,5). Mithra is said to move through all the seven continents (karshvares) of Earth (16). He is created by Ahura Mazda "possessing the most xwarenah of the supernatural gods" (Zamyad Yasht, 35), and is represented as bestowing the xvarenah upon all the seven continents (Mihir Yasht, 16).

Mithra moves in a chariot driven by "four stallions" (124-5) and is represented as a god of war (35-43). The solar force is originally invested with this martial virtue since, as we have seen, it has to battle the demons of darkness in order to maintain its glory. Mithra is also supposed to have a "thousand eyes" (or "spies") (82) with which he observes and judges the actions of man. Mithra is accompanied in his circuits by Sraosha (Faith) and Rashnu (Justice) (41).[97] Mitra is the one who acts as judge among the gods, since he oversees the universe. In the Indic *Mahābhārata* IX,44,5, too Mitra is accompanied by two companions, Suvrata (true to his vows) and Satyasamdha (true to his contracts), corresponding to the Iranian Sraosha and Rashu.

Among the Romans, **Mars**[98] is normally associated with war but was originally an agricultural

---

[97] In Srosh Yasht, Sraosha is called "the incarnate Word". In Vedic literature, Sūrya's daughter is called Shraddhā (Faith), according to *SB* XII,vii,3,11.

[98] The original form of Mars may have been *Mas*, meaning male and implying virility (see Isidore of Seville, *Etymologiae*, 5,33,5).

Fig. 9 - Mithra.

deity.[99] Indeed, Maurus Servius Honoratus, in his 'Commentary on the *Aeneid* of Vergil,' contrasts Mars with Quirinus: 'When he rampages, Mars is called *Gradivus*, but when he's at peace *Quirinus*.' This is rather like the verse in *RV* V,3,1 where Varuna is distinguished from Mitra: "Thou at thy birth art Varuna, O Agni; when thou art kindled thou becomest Mitra." So Mars Quirinus may be equated with Varuna and Mars Gradivus with Mitra. However, Mitra in the Vedas is not a god of war but of peace and justice. Both Mitra and Varuna are represented conjointly by the Maitrāvaruna priests, who are assistants of the Rigvedic Hotr priests. In *RV* VII, 82,5 and *RV* VI,68,3,[100] quoted above, Mitra is also contrasted with Indra, where Mitra has a quiet brāhmanical nature compared to the kshatriya Indra.

The original character of the Roman Mars may have been that of Quirinus guarding the peace of the Roman nation,[101] though he was adopted by the Roman military in his warlike qualities borrowed in part from the Greek God of war, Ares and, thus, the Indo-Āryan Indra. Ares is the same as Verethraghna since Verethraghna is designated on the tomb of King Antiochos I as "Artagnes, Herakles, Ares" (P. Kretschmer, "Indra und der hethitische Gott Inaras," *Kleinasiatische Forschungen I* (1930), p.313). It may be noted also that the Middle Persian version of

---

[99] Wouter Belier has discussed the agricultural orgins of Mars in his *Decayed Gods: Origin and Development of Georges Dumézil's 'idéologie tripartie'*, Leiden: Brill, 1991.

[100] See above p.23.

[101] See Isidore of Seville, *Etymologiae*, 5,33,5 (see also Wouter Belier, *op.cit.*, p.88).

Verethraghna, Bahram, is associated with the planet
Mars.[102]

Fig. 10 - Mars Ultor, Forum of Nerva, 1st c. A.D.

---

[102]   See R.C. Zaehner, Zurvan: *A Zoroastrian Dilemma*, Oxford:
Clarendon Press, 1955, pp.147ff.

Dumézil believed that Mars was primarily a god of war and only incidentally a god of agriculture or civic peace.[103] But it is clear that Dumézil's higher evaluation of the first two priestly orders representing the magical power of Diespiter and the warlike bravery of Mars in comparison with the last order of Quirinus representing fertility, prosperity and the 'people' generally is erroneous since Mars Quirinus (Varuna) and Mars Gradivus (Mitra) are the same solar force.[104] Sociological studies of Roman religion ignore the continuity of the solar force that forms the sun. Quirinus (Varuna) does not represent the third caste but is the same Agni that develops into Gradivus (Mars), a counterpart of Indra. It is important to remember also that all three Roman deities, Quirinus, Mars and Diespiter, had their own *flamines,* who are counterparts of the Indic brāhmans.[105]

---

[103] See G. Dumézil, *Archaic Roman Religion*, Part I, Ch.2.

[104] See, for instance, G. Dumézil, *op. cit.*, pp.156, 161.

[105] In his study *Mitra-Varuna: Essai sur deux representations indo-européenes de la souveraineté*, Paris: Gallimard, 1948, Chs. I-II, Dumézil introduces another distinction between *flamines* and *luperci* and between brāhmans and gandharvas, the former associated with Mitra and the latter with Varuna. But the gandharvas are entirely mythological figures and not a social caste such as the brāhmanical.

III.
ĀDITYA-HVARE-DIESPITER

The final perfection of the universe that has emerged in the Mid-region between Earth and Heaven is the sun of the heavens. The source of this third birth of Agni is, in the Vedas, said to be the waters surrounding Earth as well as in the Mid-Region of our universe. In *KYV* IV,2,2, it is stated that

> In the waters thirdly [was Agni born] the manly
> The Manly souled [Indra-Soma] kindleth thee in the ocean, in the waters,
> In the breast of the sky, O Agni, he who gazeth on men.
> Thee [Agni] standing in the third region,
> In the birthplace of holy order [Rta], the steers [Mitra-Varuna] inspirited.

The third region is the mid-Region of our universe, and the form of Agni as the one "who gazeth on men" is that of the sun-god of the heavens called Āditya (son of Aditi, the personified waters surrounding Earth) or Sūrya. At *RV* X,72,7, the sun is said to be born of the waters and located in the highest heaven, surrounded by the waters.[106]

In the *Atharva Veda* IV,10,5, the sun is said to be "born from the ocean, born from Vrtra."[107] The slaying of Vrtra by Indra not only forms heaven and earth out of the latter's body but also allows the elevation of the sun to the mid-region between them: "As you, Indra, killed Vrtra with power, you raised the sun in heaven to be seen" (*RV* I,51,4). According to *RV* X,121,7, it is Indra's deliverance of the waters from the grasp of Vrtra and their subsequent outflow which allow the waters to give birth to Agni (i.e., his third form as the sun). The waters, which are clearly related to seminal fluid, flow out as seven cosmic streams which are called "mothers" (*RV* II,12,3; X,17,10; VIII,96,1), who guard the birth of Shiva's solar son, Skanda (Dravidian: Muruga).

The vital solar energy rises from the depths of the Abyss in this flood, since Indra/Soma is said in *RV* IX,42,1 to engender the sun in "floods" along with the other stars. Thus, the flood is the result of the splitting of the universe as well as the condition of the creation of its light.

The final identification of Indra with the sun of the heavens is seen in several passages of the *RV*.[108] Indra is the hero who facilitates the birth of our universe as well as releases the solar energy from the icy forces of resistance represented by the Panis and Vrtra. In *RV* II,21,4 the sun is said to be fixed in our

---

[106]   See W. Kirfel, *Die Kosmographie der Inder*, Hildesheim: G. Olms, 1967, p.14f.

[107]   Cf. *SB* V,v,5,1-5.

[108]   See, for instance, *RV* VIII,6,24,30; I,83,5; III,39,7; VIII,69,2; X,55,3; X,111,7.

heavens by Indra. In *RV* IX,63,8, Indra is said to make the sun move by yoking ten coursers to it.

In *RV* I,24,8, the path of the sun in the system is said to be ordained by Varuna himself. The sun is set in motion (*RV* VII,86,1) and established in its course (*RV* VII, 87,1) by Varuna. At *RV* I, 1145,5 the sun of the Heavens, Sūrya, is said to be the manifest form of Varuna. When the sun sets, it is said to become one with Varuna (*KB* XVIII,9). In *RV* VII,99,4 Sūrya (Āditya, the sun of heaven), Dawn (representing the sun of the mid-region, or Vāyu) and Agni (representing the sun of earth) are said to be the children of Vishnu. In *AV* XIII,3,13 the different forms of the sun of our system are described in the following manner:

> This Agni becomes Varuna in the evening; in the morning, rising he becomes Mitra; he, having become Savitar, goes through the atmosphere; he, having become Indra, burns through the midst of the sky.

Among the Iranians, the sun of the heavens is called **Hvare**, which is the Avestan form of Svar (the shining one), another name of Sūrya.[109]

The Hurrian version of the Indo-Iranian Mitra/Mithra is **Shimige** who, like the Hittite sun-god, is represented as riding on a bull. This may be a local adaptation of the familiar Iranian Mithraic iconography. The god-lists in the Hittite treaties[110] begin with the heavenly form of the sun, dUTU SAME/ nepisas, the **Sun-god of Heaven**. This is the

---

[109] The Hittite/Hurrian form of Sūrya is Suwalliyat.

[110] See D. Yoshida, *Untersuchungen*, pp.12-29.

solar light that reigns in heaven after rising from the waters as the sun-god of the waters. Muwattalli's prayer in KUB VI 45 III, 13ff. addressed to the sun-god of the heavens runs: "you rise, sun-god of heaven, from the waters, and enter heaven."[111]

Among the Greeks, **Apollo**, the son of Zeus and Leto, is the equivalent of the Indic Sūrya. However, in Hellenistic times,[112] Apollo was identified with **Helios,** the son of the Titans, Hyperion and Theia,[113] who is the solar force in its earlier form. Helios is represented as driving a chariot drawn by solar steeds called "fire-darting steeds" by Pindar (*Olympian Odes* 7,71).[114]

Among the Romans, **Diespiter**, Father Heaven, represents the highest god and is, therefore, the equivalent of Āditya. Since he is the same as Purusha/Brahman/Indra we see that the appearance of the sun signals the manifestation of the highest form of the divine Fire in our universe. The priests of Diespiter, the *flamines dialis*, were, accordingly, the highest of the three priestly orders in ancient Rome, a fact amply demonstrated by Dumézil in his study of ancient Roman religion.

We see, therefore, that the most significant trinity among the ancient Indo-Āryans, Agni-Vāyu-Āditya, is one that represents the forms that the cosmic

---

[111]   See E. Tenner, *op.cit.*, p.186.

[112]   See Pseudo-Eratosthenes, *Catasterismi*, 24.

[113]   Hesiod, *Theogony*, 371.

[114]   The Indic Sūrya too drives a chariot drawn by seven bay steeds (*RV* I,50,8).

Fig. 11 - Apollo Belvedere, 2nd c. A.D.

fire takes in the underworld of Earth before it is installed as the sun in the Heaven of our universe. This is not a sociological trinity as Dumézil's studies would lead one to believe. The social caste and class systems noticeable in various ancient Indo-European societies are based on the human microcosmic correspondences to the various psychological qualities embodied in the different parts of the primordial macrocosmic Purusha, whose fallen fiery essence is the source of our sun. We have seen that the gods, who represent the various stages of the development of our sun, are not restricted to any of the Indian castes, though a couple of them may be described as being brāhmanical or kshatriya in character. A closer focus on the cosmological insights that inform ancient Indo-European religions should, therefore, serve to correct the misleading sociological orientations that Dumézilian comparative mythology has promoted.

EPILOGUE

Since the solar cosmology of the Indo-Europeans is traceable in more or less similar forms among the ancient Indians, Iranians, Hittites, Greeks, and Romans, we may briefly consider the course of the Indo-European migrations following the euhemeristic account of Snorri Sturluson,[115] the author of the thirteenth century *Prose Edda*. According to Sturluson, the Germans and Scandinavians derived their religion from Anatolians who moved into Europe.[116] The leader

---

[115] See *The Prose Edda*, Prologue, tr. A.G. Brodeur, London: OUP, 1916.

[116] This is confirmed by the earliest archaeology of Europe, where the first formation of the earliest Germanic cultures is to be located in the south, in modern day Czechoslovakia, which it may have reached from "the Mediterranean or Anatolia" (G. Childe, *The Dawn of European Civilization*, London: Routledge and Kegan Paul Ltd., 1961., p.101). Geoffrey of Monmouth (*History of the Kings of Britain*, Chs.3-16) points to the Trojan origin of even the earliest Britons, since Britain was, according to him, first settled by a great grandson of Aeneas called Brute.

of the Anatolians (the "Aesir") was called Odin (the Scandinavian form of the German 'Wotan'). In the *Prose Edda*, 'Gylfaginning,' ch.6, the Primordial Man, equivalent of the Indic Purusha, is called Ymir, and he has a son called Búri whose grandsons were Odin, Vili, and Ve. Odin originally lived with Ymir in the Elder Asgard, which is the primal cosmos understood in a geographical manner.

Following Sturluson's narratives in the *Heimskringla*, we may surmise that the originators of the Odin/Wotan mythology were first located east of the Don. According to the first section of *Heimskringla* called 'Ynglingasaga,' ch.1, Odin's original homeland was east of the Don river, the river in Russia that flows into the Sea of Azov, the north-eastern extension of the Black Sea. The Don itself

> was formerly called Tanakvísl (fork of the Don) or Vanakvísl (fork of the Vanir). It reaches the sea in Svartahaf.[117]

The land around the Don delta was the land of the rivals of the Aesir, the Vanir:

> The land within Vanakvíslir (delta of the Don) was then called Vanaland (Land of Vanir) or Vanaheimr (World of Vanir). This river separates the thirds of the world. The region to the east is called Asia, that to the west, Europe.

---

[117]　Snorri Sturluson, *Heimkringsla*, Vol.I, tr. A. Finlay and A. Faulkes, London: Viking Society for Northern Research, 2011.

East of Vanaland was Ásaland (Land of the Æsir) or Ásaheimr (World of the Æsir). The capital city of Asaheimr was called Ásgarðr (ch.2):

> To the east of Tanakvísl in Asia it was called Ásaland (Land of the Æsir) or Ásaheimr (World of the Æsir), and the capital city that was in the land they called Ásgarðr. And in that town was the ruler who was called Óðinn. There was a great place of worship there. It was the custom there that twelve temple priests were of highest rank. They were in charge of the worship and judgements among people. They are known as díar or lords. They were to receive service and veneration from all people.

Now, the earliest cultures **north of the Black Sea**, those of the Pontic-Caspian Steppe, are the Sintashta (2100-1800 B.C.) and the Andronovo (2000-900 B.C.), both associated with the **Indo-Iranian**, or Āryan, culture. So, we may assume that both the Aesir and the Vanir belonged to this predominant group. The battle between the Aesir and the Vanir may reflect the beginning of the split between the Indian and Iranian branches of the Āryan tribes since the Iranians, especially by the time of the Zoroastrian reform, worshipped only the Asuras and considered the Daevas as demons. However, the language spoken by the Aesir and Vanir may have been the original Indo-Iranian since even the Āryan Mitanni, who appeared in south-eastern Anatolia and northern Syria in the 16th century B.C. exhibit elements of both branches of the Indo-Iranian language.[118]

In the *Prose Edda*, 'Gylfaginning,' 9, Asgard is the name of Heaven, and is said to have been constructed after the killing and dismembering of Ymir. Odin and his brothers then fashion the human race out of two trees, a male child called Ask and the other a female called Embla. The gods and their semi-divine human offspring then dwell in Asgard, which is represented terrestrially as being located **south of the Black Sea**, in Anatolia:

> Next they made for themselves in the middle of the world a city which is called Ásgard; men call it **Troy**. There dwelt the gods and their kindred;[119]

Asgard is firmly identified with Troy and glorified in its opulence:

> Near the earth's centre was made that goodliest of homes and haunts that ever have been, which is called Troy, even that which we call Turkland. This abode was much more gloriously made than others, and fashioned with more skill of craftsmanship in manifold

---

[118]   Several Median words are traceable in Old Persian (see P.O. Skjaervo, in G.Erdosy, (ed.) *The Indo-Aryans of Ancient South Asia*, Berlin: Walter de Gruyter, 1995, p.159). That the term 'Mede' might be related to the term 'Mitanni' was suggested early by J. Charpentier, "The Date of Zoroaster," *BSOS* 3 (1923-25), 747-55, among others.

[119]   Snorri Sturluson, *The Prose Edda*, tr. A.G. Brodeur, London: OUP, 1916.

wise, both in luxury and in the wealth which was there in abundance. There were twelve kingdoms and one High King, and many sovereignties belonged to each kingdom; in the stronghold were twelve chieftains.

———

The chief of the Aesir, Wotan, and his people eventually migrated to the German lands:

> And wherever they went over the lands of the earth, many glorious things were spoken of them, so that they were held more like gods than men. They made no end to their journeying till they were come north into the land that is now called **Saxland**;[120] there Odin tarried for a long space, and took the land into his own hand, far and wide.

Odin's three sons, Vegdeg, Beldeg (Baldur), and Sigi ruled over **East Germany, Westphalia, and France**, respectively. Further expeditions took Odin to **Denmark, Sweden, and Norway**. In the process of these migrations the Aesirs mingled with the local peoples and thereby succeeded in spreading the "language of Asia" all over Europe:

> The Aesir took wives of the land for themselves, and some also for their sons; and these kindreds became many in number, so

---

[120]   Saxony.

that throughout Saxland, and thence all over
the region of the north, they spread out until
their tongue, even the speech of the men of
Asia, was the native tongue over all these
lands.

The date of the Odinic migration may have been
around that of the Trojan War (ca.12th century B.C.).

Odin is endowed with quasi-magical powers, as
Sturluson recounts in the 'Ynglingasaga,' ch.6:

But there is this to be said about why he was
so very exalted—there were these reasons for
it: he was so fair and noble in countenance
when he was sitting among his friends that it
rejoiced the hearts of all. But when he went to
battle he appeared ferocious to his enemies.
And the reason was that he had the faculty of
changing complexion and form in whatever
manner he chose. Another was that he spoke
so eloquently and smoothly that everyone who
heard thought that only what he said was true.
Everything he said was in rhyme, like the way
what is now called poetry is composed. He
and his temple priests were called craftsmen of
poems, for that art originated with them in the
Northern lands.

Not only did he introduce the poetic art into the
lands that the Aesir settled, but he also established
the laws of Anatolia in the north:

he chose for himself the site of a city which
is now called Sigtun. There he established

chieftains in the fashion which had prevailed in Troy; he set up also twelve head-men to be doomsmen over the people and to judge the laws of the land; and he ordained also all laws as there had been before in Troy, and according to the customs of the Turks.

Odin's fellow Aesir include Baldr ('Gylfaginning' ch.22), Tyr, Bragi, Heimdallr, Hodr, Vidarr, and Loki (chs.25ff.). Thor is another Aesir (ch.21), and he is loosely identified with Hector, the Trojan prince just as Loki is identified with Ulysses, the Greek (ch.54). In the Prologue to the *Prose Edda*, "Tror," or "Thor," is the son of a Trojan king called Mennon or Munon who had married a daughter of King Priam. He is said to have been brought up in **Thrace**, which is the domain of Dionysus. In the 'Ynglingasaga,' ch.5, Thor is represented as one of the Aesir appointed as priests in the northern lands after their colonisation by Odin. It may be noted that in the 'Prologue' to the *Prose Edda* – unlike in 'Gylfaginning' – Voden (Wotan) or Odin is said to be a distant descendant of Thor. But this may be explained by the fact that, although the Wotan of Asgard appears in the universal Tree of Life later than Thor, whose battling of the serpent precedes the full rise of the Tree, Wotan (Vāyu) is already a major god in the Elder Asgard (the primal cosmos).

If we attempt to ascertain the linguistic affinities of the culture imported into Europe by the Aesir of Anatolia, we have to choose between the shatem Mitanni and the centum Hittite languages as the two likely ancestors of the Germanic languages (which are centum languages). While the Hittites were

Indo-Europeans who ruled in central Anatolia in the 17th century B.C., their religious culture is heavily dependent on that of the earlier non-Indo-European Hattic culture of Anatolia. The name Wata, however, is reflected in the Hittite divine name, Huwattassis, for the god of Wind.[121] The Mitanni who ruled in eastern Anatolia and northern Syria in the 16th century B.C., exhibit a more Sanskritic culture since the first coherent mention of Indic gods appears in the treaty between the Mitanni-Hurrian king Šattiwaza and the Hittite king Šuppililiumas I dating from the sixteenth century B.C. and including the names Mitra-Varuna, Indra, and Nāsatyas.[122]

The collective name 'Edda' for the sacred poems of the Germanic peoples is clearly related to the Indo-Āryan 'Veda,' as well as to the Zoroastrian Iranian 'Avesta.' In the Eddic poem 'Rigsthula', Edda is given as the name of the ancestress of the human race who bears three children Thrall, Karl, and Jarl, representing serfs, freemen engaged in farming and crafts, and warrior nobles. The protagonist of the poem himself is called Rig and is identified with the god Heimdall. The juxtaposition of Rig (a word signifying radiation or glory) with Edda seems to point to Indic origins, where Rig is the first of the Vedas.

In the *Prose Edda*, 'Gylfaginning' (The Deluding of Gylfi), the end of the universe, Ragnarök, is heralded by a long winter, exactly as in the Yima

---

[121]   See E. Laroche, *Recherches sur les noms divins hittites, RHA* VII, 45 (1946-7), p.69.

[122]   CTH 51 and 52; see D. Yoshida, *Untersuchungen zu den Sonnengottheiten bei den Hethitern*, Heidelberg: Universitätsverlag C. Winter, 1996, p.12.

story of the Iranian Vendidad.[123] We have also seen that the German form of the god of Wind, Wotan, is recognisably related to the Āryan Wata, a god of Wind who is more prominently mentioned in the Iranian sacred literature than in the Indic.[124] This may suggest that the Aesir that emigrated from the Anatolian region belonged to the Indo-Iranian tribes before the separation of the Indic from the Iranian Āryans.

Furthermore, the spread of the original Indo-European religion from around the Black Sea through Anatolia, the Balkans, and Italy to the European north – as recounted by Sturluson – may have extended even to Mesopotamia, for the name of the Eddic Ocean god, Aegir, whom we have studied above, clearly resembles that of his Sumerian counterpart, Enki (Lord of Earth).[125]

---

[123]   See H. Usener, *Die Sintfluthsagen*, Bonn: Friedrich Cohen, 1899, p.208ff.

[124]   The Avesta (Yasht 14, Yasht 8) uses the form Wata to denote the more corporeal form of the god of wind Vāyu. *Rig Veda* X, 136,4 refers to "the steed of Vāta, the friend of Vāyu".

[125]   As we have seen above, Earth is the 'underworld' that is surrounded by an Ocean (Okeanos). Hence the Lord of Earth is also an Ocean-god.

LIST OF ILLUSTRATIONS

Fig.1 - Georges Dumézil (Miehs (discuție), Public domain, via Wikimedia Commons.

Fig 2. - Vitruvian_Man_by_Leonardo_da_Vinci-By Paris Orlando - Own work, CC BY-SA 4.0, https://commons.wikimedia.org/w/index.php?curid=83818167.

Fig 3. - Ganesh - Rajenver, CC BY-SA 3.0 <https://creativecommons.org/licenses/by-sa/3.0>, via Wikimedia Commons.

Fig. 4. - 8th_century_Vishnu_avatar_Vamana_taking_one_of_ three_colossal_steps_at_Virupaksha_Shaivism_temple%2C_ Pattadakal_Hindu_monuments_Karnataka.jpg Ms Sarah Welch, CC BY-SA 4.0 <https://creativecommons.org/licenses/ by-sa/4.0>, via Wikimedia Commons.

Fig. 5.- Typhon -Staatliche Antikensammlungen, Public domain, via Wikimedia Commons.

Fig. 6 - Jormangandr Lorenz Frølich, CC0, via Wikimedia Commons.

Fig.7 -The Swedish History Museum, Stockholm from Sweden, CC BY 2.0 <https://creativecommons.org/licenses/by/2.0>, via Wikimedia Commons.

Fig. 8 - Odin Lorenz Frølich, Public domain, via Wikimedia Commons - Odin sacrificing himself upon Yggdrasil (1895) by Lorenz Frølich.

Fig 9. - Iranian Mithra By dynamosquito from France - Mithra, CC BY-SA 2.0, https://commons.wikimedia.org/w/index. php?curid=32705048.

Fig 10 - Marble statue of Mars: "Pyrrhus", dated at I sec. A.D. Hight: cm 360. It was found in the Nerva's Forum, in Rome, and it's now placed in the atrium of Capitoline Museums in Rome Andrea PuggioniUploaded by Cynwolfe at en.wikipedia, CC BY 2.0 <https://creativecommons.org/licenses/by/2.0>, via Wikimedia Commons.

Fig. 11 - Apollo - Dennis Jarvis from Halifax, Canada, CC BY-SA 2.0 <https://creativecommons.org/licenses/by-sa/2.0>, via Wikimedia Commons.

OTHER BOOKS BY
ALEXANDER JACOB

THE GRAIL – TWO STUDIES

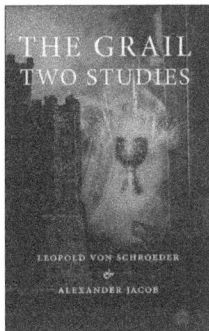

A proper understanding of the significance of the cultic object called the Holy Grail has eluded most scholars who have confined their research to western European literary and cultural sources, especially since the originally Celtic story of the Holy Grail underwent numerous bewildering metamorphoses in the romances of the Middle Ages.

It was the Indologist Leopold von Schroeder's reading of the Grail story (1910) in the light of his knowledge of Indic mythology that first achieved a dramatic expansion of the field of Holy Grail scholarship. The only other scholar who developed a comprehensive comparative mythological study of the Grail was perhaps Julius Evola in his Il *Mistero del Graal e la Tradizione Ghibellina dell'Impero* (1937).

Schroeder's fascinating elucidation of some of the key symbols of the Grail legends using his knowledge of ancient Indian literature is amplified by Alexander Jacob's reconstruction of the cosmological basis of these symbols and his analysis of the solar rituals that characterized the diverse yet related religions of the ancient Indo-Europeans.

INDO-EUROPEAN MYTHOLOGY AND RELIGION:
ESSAYS

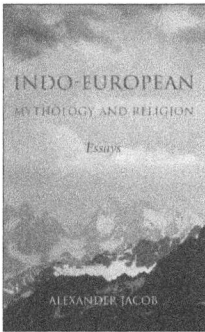

The essays presented in this collection are based on Alexander Jacob's earlier works, *Ātman: A Reconstruction of the Solar Cosmology of the Indo-Europeans*, Hildesheim: Georg Olms, 2005 and *Brahman: A Study of the Solar Rituals of the Indo-Europeans*, Hildesheim: Georg Olms, 2012. They expand on the cosmological and religious themes discussed in these books with special reference to the origins and development of the Indic and European spiritual traditions. Those familiar with the earlier works will not be surprised that Dr. Jacob's view of the term 'Indo-European' is rather more comprehensive than the more restricted term 'Āryan' that has hitherto been widely used as a synonym of it. And those interested in the Āryan ethos itself – chiefly on account of the German use of the term during the last war – may be surprised to learn that it does not consist in nationalistic virtues so much as in spiritual discipline and development – and that this development is characteristic of the religions of very extended and diversified branches of the Indo-European family.

VEDANTA, PLATO, AND KANT
BY PAUL DEUSSEN
TRANSLATED BY ALEXANDER JACOB

"The Kantian worldview, which always underlay all religion, philosophy, and art, could not have been the eternal truth if it did not emerge more or less clearly everywhere that the human mind penetrated into the depths, as this occurred, for example, in India through the Upanishads of the Vedas and the Vedanta based on them and in Greece through Parmenides and Plato. To consider both these phenomena in the light of the Kantian philosophy is the task that we have set ourselves here." - *Paul Deussen*

Vedanta, Plato, and Kant is a new translation. The book presents a defense of Shankara's Advaita Vedānta philosophy as well as an elucidation of the Greek Idealistic doctrines of Parmenides and Plato. In all these schools of thought, Deussen detects a similar basic understanding of the world as a mere appearance distinct from Ideal Reality. He approximated this understanding to the Kantian notion of 'things in themselves' (Dinge-an-sich) and noted a degeneration of the original Vedic and Upanishadic worldview in the philosophies that followed, such as the Sāmkhya and Buddhism, just as there was a corruption of Parmenides' doctrine of Being in the philosophy of his pupil Zeno. Similarly, he believes that Kant's revolutionary Idealistic insights in Germany were also distorted by the post-Kantian thinkers and not generally understood in their original form except by Arthur Schopenhauer (1788-1860), who developed the doctrine of the world as a mere representation produced by the innate intuitive forms within the Intellect – Space, Time, and Causality.

Includes a preface by Alexander Jacob (Translator).